Let's explore Europe!

Hello! Welcome to Europe!

We come from different countries and speak different languages, but this continent is the home we share.

Come with us and let's explore Europe together! It will be an adventurous journey through time and space and you'll find out loads of interesting things.

As we go along, test yourself to see how much you've learnt. Go to our website **europa.eu/kids-corner** where you will find the Let's explore Europe! game and many other quizzes and games about Europe.

At school, explore further! Ask your teacher to tell you more about each of the topics in this book. Then do some deeper research in the school library or on the Internet.
You could even write your own booklet about what you have discovered.

Ready? Then let's begin!

1

What's in this book?

A continent to discover

Europe is one of the world's seven continents. The others are Africa, North and South America, Antarctica, Asia and Australia/Oceania.

Europe stretches all the way from the Arctic in the north to the Mediterranean Sea in the south, and from the Atlantic Ocean in the west to the Ural mountains (in Russia) in the east. It has many rivers, lakes and mountain ranges. The map on page 4 tells you the names of some of the biggest ones.

The highest mountain in Europe is Mount Elbrus, in the Caucasus mountains, on the border between Russia and Georgia. Its highest peak is 5 642 metres above sea level.

The highest mountain in western Europe is Mont Blanc, in the Alps, on the border between France and Italy. Its summit is over 4 800 metres above sea level.

Also in the Alps is Lake Geneva – the largest freshwater lake in western Europe. It lies between France and Switzerland, goes as deep as 310 metres and holds about 89 trillion litres of water.

The largest lake in central Europe is Balaton, in Hungary. It is 77 kilometres (km) long and covers an area of about 600 square kilometres (km^2). Northern Europe has even bigger lakes, including Saimaa in Finland (1 147 km^2) and Vänern in Sweden (more than 5 500 km^2). The largest lake in Europe as a whole is Lake Ladoga. It is located in north-western Russia and it is the 14th largest lake in the world. Its surface covers an area of 17 700 km^2.

Mount Elbrus, the highest mountain in Europe.

Lake Geneva, in the Alps.

Lake Saimaa, in Finland.

The continent of Europe

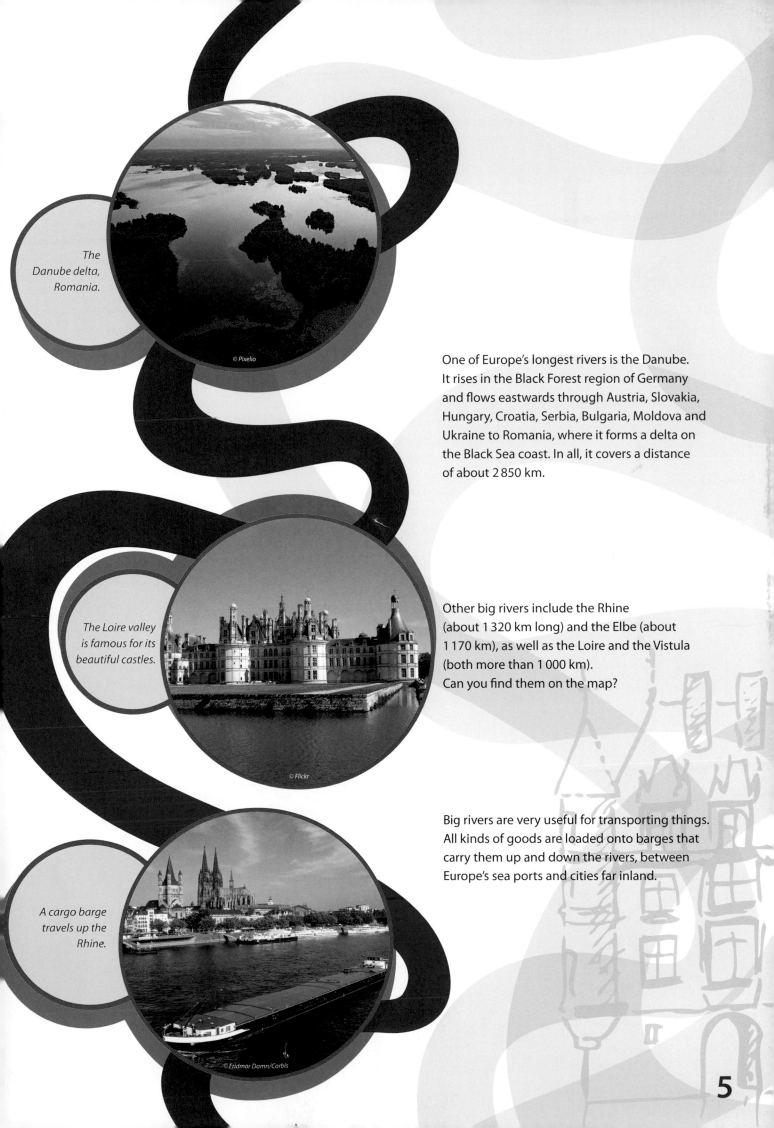

The Danube delta, Romania.

© Pixelio

The Loire valley is famous for its beautiful castles.

© Flickr

A cargo barge travels up the Rhine.

© Fridmar Damn/Corbis

One of Europe's longest rivers is the Danube. It rises in the Black Forest region of Germany and flows eastwards through Austria, Slovakia, Hungary, Croatia, Serbia, Bulgaria, Moldova and Ukraine to Romania, where it forms a delta on the Black Sea coast. In all, it covers a distance of about 2 850 km.

Other big rivers include the Rhine (about 1 320 km long) and the Elbe (about 1 170 km), as well as the Loire and the Vistula (both more than 1 000 km).
Can you find them on the map?

Big rivers are very useful for transporting things. All kinds of goods are loaded onto barges that carry them up and down the rivers, between Europe's sea ports and cities far inland.

Getting around

Stephenson's 'Rocket'.

Did you know that railways were invented in Europe? It was in England that George Stephenson introduced the first passenger train in 1825. His most famous locomotive was called 'the Rocket' and it reached speeds of more than 40 kilometres per hour (km/h) – which was really fast for those days.

Today, Europe's high-speed electric trains are very different from those first steam engines. They are very comfortable and they travel at speeds of up to 330 km/h on specially built tracks. More tracks are being built all the time, to allow people to travel quickly between Europe's big cities.

Roads and railways sometimes have to cross mountain ranges, wide rivers or even the sea. So engineers have built some very long bridges and tunnels. The longest road tunnel in Europe is the Laerdal tunnel in Norway, between Bergen and Oslo. It is more than 24 km long and was opened in the year 2000.

The longest railway tunnel in Europe is the Channel Tunnel. It carries Eurostar high-speed trains under the sea between Calais in France and Folkestone in England, and it's more than 50 km long.

Folkestone

Calais

Folkestone

Calais

Eurostar trains at
St Pancras station (London).

© Colin Garratt/Corbis

The highest bridge in the world (245 metres tall) is the Millau Viaduct in France, which was opened in 2004.

Two of the longest bridges in Europe are the Oresund road and rail bridge (16 km long) between Denmark and Sweden and the Vasco da Gama road bridge (more than 17 km long) across the river Tagus in Portugal. The Vasco da Gama bridge is named after a famous explorer, and you can read about him in the chapter 'A journey through time'.

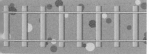

The world's highest bridge – the Millau Viaduct (France).

The fastest ever passenger plane, the Concorde.

The world's biggest passenger plane – the Airbus A380.

People also travel around Europe by plane, because air travel is quick. Some of the world's best planes are built in Europe – for example, the 'Airbus'. Different European countries make different parts of an Airbus, and then a team of engineers puts the whole plane together.

The fastest ever passenger plane, the Concorde, was designed by a team of French and British engineers. Concorde could fly at 2 160 km/h – twice the speed of sound – and could cross the Atlantic in less than three hours! (Most planes take about eight hours.) Concorde took its final flight in 2003.

Faster than any plane are space rockets, such as Ariane – a joint project between several European countries. People don't travel in the Ariane rocket: it is used to launch satellites, which are needed for TV and mobile phone networks, for scientific research and so on. Many of the world's satellites are now launched using these European rockets.

The success of Concorde, Airbus and Ariane show what can be achieved when European countries work together.

Languages in Europe

People in Europe speak many different languages. Most of these languages belong to three large groups or 'families': Germanic, Slavic and Romance.

The languages in each group share a family likeness because they are descended from the same ancestors. For example, Romance languages are descended from Latin – the language spoken by the Romans.

Here's how to say 'Good morning' or 'Hello' in just a few of these languages.

Germanic

Danish	Godmorgen
Dutch	Goedemorgen
English	Good morning
German	Guten Morgen
Swedish	God morgon

Romance

French	Bonjour
Italian	Buongiorno
Portuguese	Bom dia
Romanian	Bună dimineața
Spanish	Buenos días

Slavic

Bulgarian	Dobró útro
Croatian	Dobro jutro
Czech	Dobré ráno
Polish	Dzień dobry
Slovak	Dobré ráno
Slovene	Dobro jutro

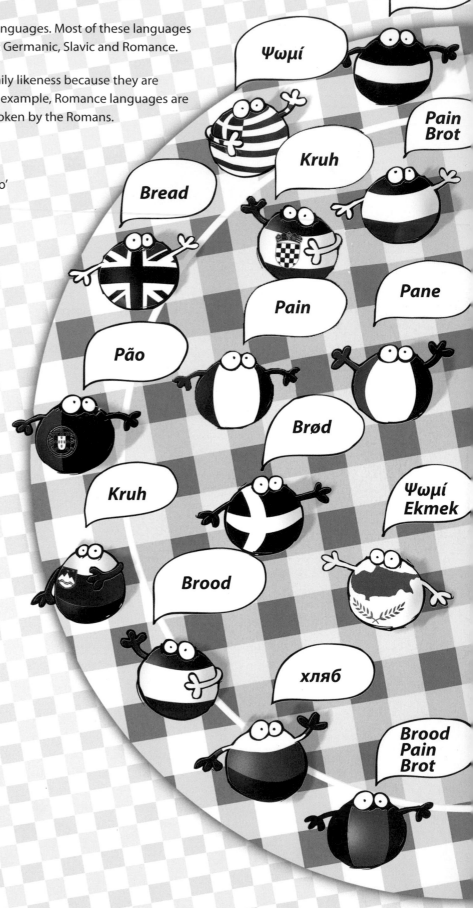

8

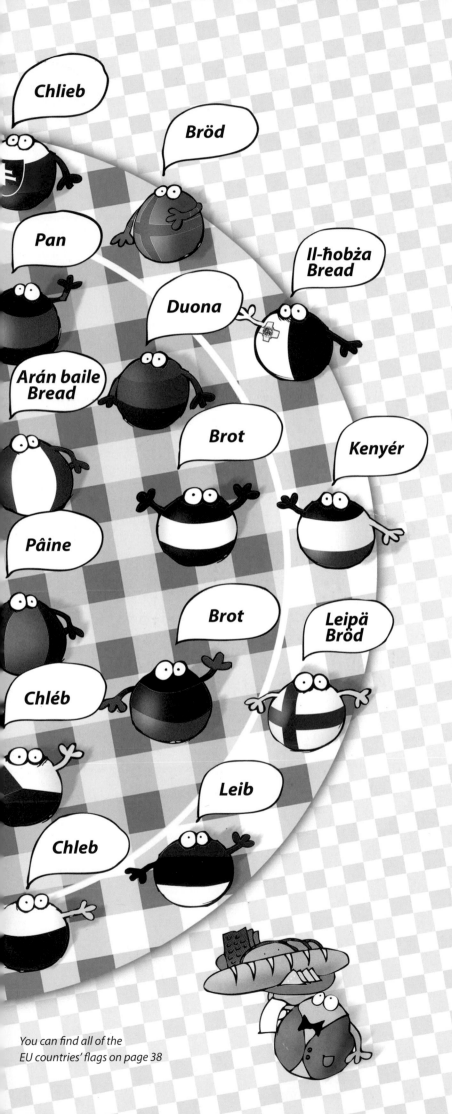

It's not hard to see the family likeness in these examples. But there are other European languages that are less closely related, or not at all related, to one another.

Here's how to say 'Good morning' or 'Hello' in several of these languages.

Basque	Egun on
Breton	Demat
Catalan	Bon dia
Estonian	Tere hommikust
Finnish	Hyvää huomenta
Gaelic (Scottish)	Madainn mhath
Greek	Kalimera
Hungarian	Jó reggelt
Irish	Dia dhuit
Latvian	Labrīt
Lithuanian	Labas rytas
Maltese	L-Għodwa t-Tajba
Welsh	Bore da

In the language of the Roma people, who live in many parts of Europe, 'Good morning' is *Lasho dyes*.

Learning languages can be great fun – and it's important on a continent like ours. Many of us enjoy going on holiday to other European countries, and getting to know the people there. That's a great opportunity to practise the phrases we know in different languages.

You can find all of the EU countries' flags on page 38

Climate and nature

Most of Europe has a 'temperate' climate – neither too hot nor too cold. The coldest places are in the far north and in the high mountains. The warmest places are in the far south and south-east.

The weather is warmest and driest in summer (roughly June to September) and coldest in winter (roughly December to March).

Europe had record-breaking hot summers in 2006 and 2010. Is this a sign that the climate is changing? Climate change is a worldwide problem that can only be solved if all countries work together.

Coping with the winter

Wild animals in cold regions usually have thick fur or feathers to keep them warm, and their coats may be white to camouflage them in the snow. Some spend the winter sleeping to save energy. This is called hibernating.

The Arctic fox ...

©Klaus Hackenberg/Corbis

European brown bears live in the mountains, where they spend the winter sleeping.

Many species of birds live on insects, small water creatures or other food that cannot easily be found during cold winter months. So they fly south in the autumn and don't return until spring. Some travel thousands of kilometres, across the Mediterranean Sea and the Sahara Desert, to spend the winter in Africa. This seasonal travelling is called migrating.

Enjoying the spring and summer

When spring comes to Europe (March to May), the weather gets warmer. Snow and ice melt. Baby fish and insect larvae swarm in the streams and ponds. Migrating birds return to make their nests and raise their families. Flowers open, and bees carry pollen from one plant to another.

Trees put out new leaves which catch the sunlight and use its energy to make the tree grow. In mountain regions, farmers move their cows up into the high meadows, where there is now plenty of fresh grass.

Even flamingos come to Europe in spring.

Summer is good in the mountain meadows.

© Aleaimage

11

Cold-blooded animals such as reptiles also need the sun to give them energy. In summer, especially in southern Europe, you will often see lizards basking in the sunshine and hear the chirping of grasshoppers and cicadas.

Lizards love warm weather.

Wasps love fruit too!

Autumn: a time of change

In late summer and autumn, the days grow shorter and the nights cooler. Many delicious fruits ripen at this time of year, and farmers are kept busy harvesting them. Nuts too ripen in autumn, and squirrels will gather and store heaps of them ready for the winter.

©Peter Bohot/Pixelio
Squirrels store nuts for their winter food.

Many trees shed their leaves in autumn because there is no longer enough sunshine for the leaves to be useful. They gradually change from green to shades of yellow, red, gold and brown. Then they fall, carpeting the ground with colour. The fallen leaves decay, enriching the soil and providing food for future generations of plant life.

This yearly cycle of the seasons, and the changes it brings, make the European countryside what it is – beautiful, and very varied.

Autumn carpets the woods with colour.

Farming

On high mountains and in the far north of Europe, farming is impossible because it is too cold for crops to grow. But evergreen trees such as pines and firs can survive cold winters. That is why Europe's coldest places are covered with evergreen forests. People use the wood from these forests to make many things – from houses and furniture to paper and cardboard packaging.

Further south, most of the land is suitable for farming. It produces a wide variety of crops including wheat, maize, sugar beet, potatoes and all sorts of fruit and vegetables.

Where there is plenty of sunshine and hardly any frost (near the Mediterranean, for example), farmers can grow fruit such as oranges and lemons, grapes and olives. Olives contain oil which can be squeezed out of the fruit and used in preparing food. Grapes are squeezed to get the juice, which can be turned into wine. Europe is famous for its very good wines, which are sold all over the world.

These grapes will be made into red wine.

Mediterranean farmers also grow lots of other fruit and vegetables. Tomatoes, for example, ripen well in the southern sunshine. But vegetables need plenty of water, so farmers in hot, dry regions will often have to irrigate their crops. That means giving them water from rivers or from under the ground.

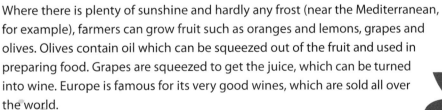

Crops in dry regions need irrigating.

Sheep grazing on grasslands.

Pigs can be kept indoors.

Grass grows easily where there is enough rain, even if the soil is shallow or not very fertile. Many European farmers keep animals that eat grass – such as cows, sheep or goats. They provide milk, meat and other useful products like wool and leather.

Many farmers also keep pigs or chickens. These animals can be raised almost anywhere because they can be kept indoors and given specially prepared feed. Chickens provide not only meat but eggs too, and some farms produce thousands of eggs every day.

Farms in Europe range from very big to very small. Some have large fields – which makes it easy to harvest crops using big machines. Others, for example in hilly areas, may have small fields. Walls or hedgerows between fields help stop the wind and rain from carrying away soil, and they can be good for wildlife too.

Many city people like to spend weekends and holidays in the European countryside, enjoying the scenery, the peace and quiet and the fresh air. We all need to do what we can to look after the countryside and keep it beautiful.

The countryside is for everyone to enjoy.

The sea

Europe has thousands and thousands of kilometres of coastline, which nature has shaped in various ways. There are tall rocky cliffs and beaches of sand or colourful pebbles formed by the sea as it pounds away at the rocks, century after century.

In Norway, glaciers have carved the coast into steep-sided valleys called fjords. In some other countries, the sea and wind pile up the sand into dunes. The highest dune in Europe (117 metres tall) is the Dune du Pyla, near Arcachon in France.

Many kinds of fish and other animals live in the sea around Europe's coasts. They provide food for sea birds, and for marine mammals such as seals. Where rivers flow into the sea, flocks of waders come to feed, at low tide, on creatures that live in the mud.

The puffin nests on cliffs, and dives to catch fish.

The sea shaped these chalk cliffs.

A glacier carved this fjord.

One of Europe's rarest animals – the monk seal – lives in the Mediterranean.

The Pyla sand dune – Europe's tallest.

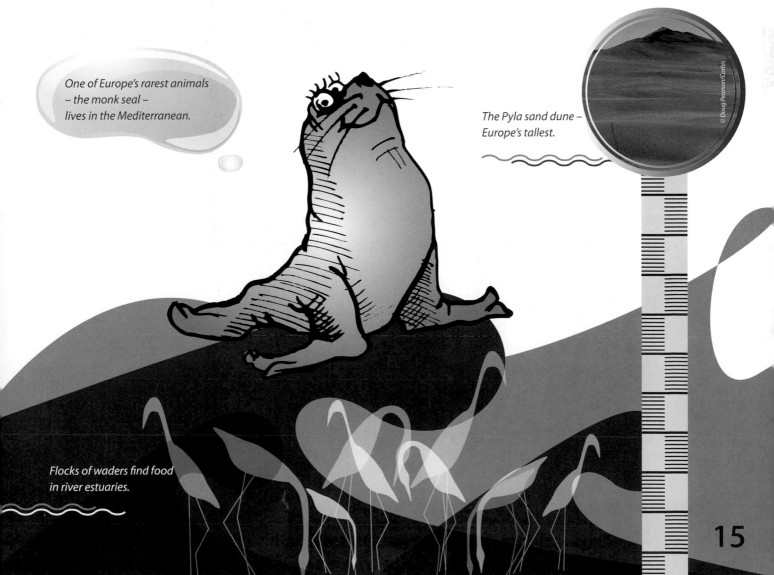

Flocks of waders find food in river estuaries.

15

People and the sea

The sea is important for people too. The Mediterranean was so important to the Romans that they called it Mare nostrum: 'our sea'. Down through the centuries, Europeans have sailed the world's oceans, discovered the other continents, explored them, traded with them and made their homes there. In the chapter 'A journey through time' you can find out more about these great voyages of discovery.

Cargo boats from around the world bring all kinds of goods (often packed in containers) to Europe's busy ports. Here they are unloaded on to trains, lorries and barges. Then the ships load up with goods that have been produced here and which are going to be sold on other continents.

Container ships carry goods to and from Europe.

Some of the world's finest ships have been built in Europe. They include Queen Mary 2 – one of the biggest passenger liners in the world. She made her first transatlantic voyage in January 2004.

One of the world's biggest passenger ships – Queen Mary 2.

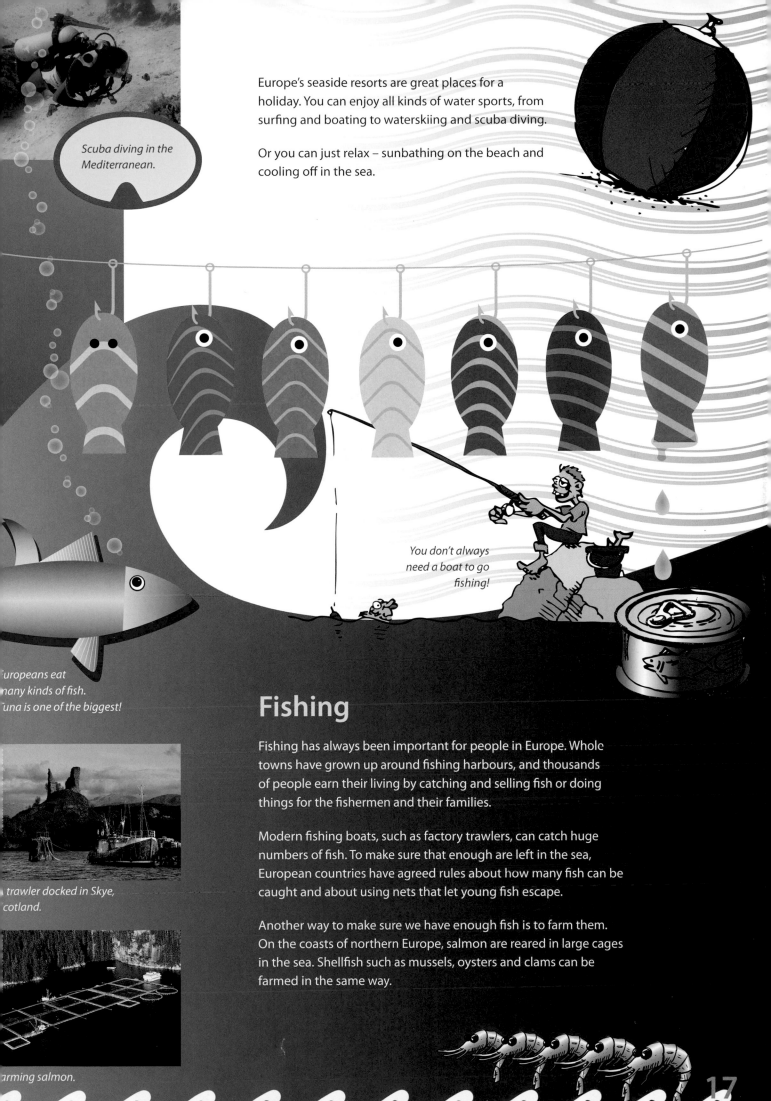

Europe's seaside resorts are great places for a holiday. You can enjoy all kinds of water sports, from surfing and boating to waterskiing and scuba diving.

Or you can just relax – sunbathing on the beach and cooling off in the sea.

Scuba diving in the Mediterranean.

You don't always need a boat to go fishing!

uropeans eat
many kinds of fish.
una is one of the biggest!

trawler docked in Skye,
cotland.

rming salmon.

Fishing

Fishing has always been important for people in Europe. Whole towns have grown up around fishing harbours, and thousands of people earn their living by catching and selling fish or doing things for the fishermen and their families.

Modern fishing boats, such as factory trawlers, can catch huge numbers of fish. To make sure that enough are left in the sea, European countries have agreed rules about how many fish can be caught and about using nets that let young fish escape.

Another way to make sure we have enough fish is to farm them. On the coasts of northern Europe, salmon are reared in large cages in the sea. Shellfish such as mussels, oysters and clams can be farmed in the same way.

Protecting Europe's coasts

Europe's coasts and the sea are important to wildlife and to people. So we need to look after them. We have to prevent them from becoming polluted by waste from factories and towns. Oil tankers sometimes have accidents, spilling huge amounts of oil into the sea. This can turn beaches black and kill thousands of seabirds.

European countries are working together to try to prevent these things from happening again and to make sure that our coastline will remain beautiful for future generations to enjoy.

A journey through time

Over thousands of years, Europe has changed enormously.
It's a fascinating story! But it's a long one, so here are just some of the highlights.

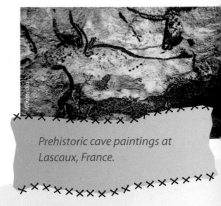

A flint tool from the Stone Age.

The Stone Age

The earliest Europeans were hunters and gatherers. On the walls of some caves they made wonderful paintings of hunting scenes. Eventually, they learnt farming and began breeding animals, growing crops and living in villages.

They made their weapons and tools from stone – by sharpening pieces of flint, for example.

Prehistoric cave paintings at Lascaux, France.

A bronze axe head.

The Bronze and Iron Ages – Learning to use metal

Several thousand years BC (before the birth of Christ), people discovered how to get different metals by heating different kinds of rock in a very hot fire. Bronze – a mixture of copper and tin – was hard enough for making tools and weapons. Gold and silver were soft but very beautiful and could be shaped into ornaments.

Later, an even harder metal was discovered: iron. The best kind of metal was steel, which was strong and didn't easily break, so it made good swords. But making steel was very tricky, so good swords were rare and valuable!

Ancient Greece

roughly 2000 to 200 BC –
BC means before the birth of Christ

In Greece about 4 000 years ago, people began to build cities. At first they were ruled by kings. Later, around 500 BC, the city of Athens introduced 'democracy' – which means 'government by the people'. (Instead of having a king, the men of Athens took decisions by voting.) Democracy is an important European invention that has spread around the world.

This Greek vase with red-figure painting dates back to around 530 BC.

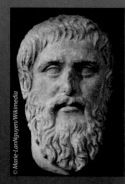

Plato, one of the world's great thinkers.

Some of the other things the ancient Greeks gave us include:

> wonderful stories about gods and heroes, wars and adventures;
> elegant temples, marble statues and beautiful pottery;
> the Olympic Games;
> well-designed theatres, and great writers whose plays are still performed today;
> teachers like Socrates and Plato, who taught people how to think logically;
> mathematicians like Euclid and Pythagoras, who worked out the patterns and rules in maths;
> scientists like Aristotle (who studied plants and animals) and Eratosthenes (who proved that the Earth is a sphere and worked out how big it is).

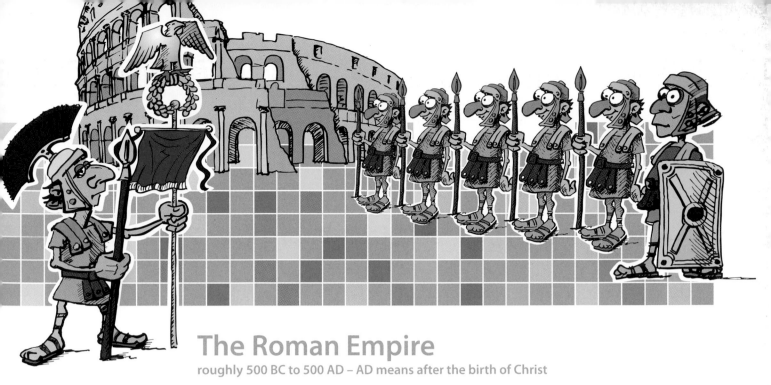

The Roman Empire
roughly 500 BC to 500 AD – AD means after the birth of Christ

Rome started out as just a village in Italy. But the Romans were very well organised, their army was very good at fighting and they gradually conquered all the lands around the Mediterranean. Eventually the Roman empire stretched all the way from northern England to the Sahara Desert and from the Atlantic to Asia.

Here are some of the things the Romans gave us:

> good, straight roads connecting all parts of the empire;
> beautiful houses with courtyards and mosaic tiled floors;
> strong bridges and aqueducts (for carrying water long distances);
> round-topped arches – which made their buildings solid and long-lasting;
> new building materials, such as cement and concrete;
> new weapons such as catapults;
> great writers like Cicero and Virgil;
> the Roman system of law, which many European countries still use today.

A Roman aqueduct still standing today: the Pont du Gard in France.

Mosaics are made using tiny pieces of stone, enamel, glass or ceramic and are used to decorate buildings.

The Middle Ages
roughly 500 to 1500 AD

When the Roman empire collapsed, different parts of Europe were taken over by different peoples. For example…

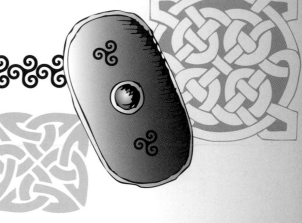

The Celts

Before Roman times, Celtic peoples lived in many parts of Europe. Their descendants today live mainly in Brittany (France), Cornwall (England), Galicia (Spain), Ireland, Scotland and Wales. In these parts of Europe, Celtic languages and culture are very much alive.

The Germanic peoples

Not all of them settled in Germany:

> **The Angles** and **Saxons** moved to England and ruled it until 1066.

> **The Franks** conquered a large part of Europe, including France, between about 500 and 800 AD. Their most famous king was Charlemagne.

> **The Goths** (Visigoths and Ostrogoths) set up kingdoms in Spain and Italy.

> **The Vikings** lived in Scandinavia. In the 800s and 900s they sailed to other countries, stealing treasure, trading and settling where there was good farmland.

The Vikings were such good sailors they even reached America (but didn't tell anyone!)

The Normans

or 'Northmen', were Vikings who settled in France (in the area we call Normandy) and then conquered England in 1066. A famous Norman tapestry shows scenes from this conquest. It is kept in a museum in the town of Bayeux.

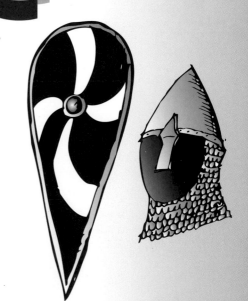

Medieval castles were built to keep out enemies.

The Slavs settled in many parts of eastern Europe and became the ancestors of today's Slavic-speaking peoples, including Belorussians, Bulgarians, Croatians, Czechs, Poles, Russians, Serbs, Slovaks, Slovenes and Ukrainians.

After **the Magyars** settled in the Carpathian Basin in the 9th and 10th centuries, they founded the Kingdom of Hungary in the year 1000. Their descendants today live in Hungary and other neighbouring countries.

During the Middle Ages, kings and nobles in Europe often quarrelled and there were many wars. (This was the time when knights in armour fought on horseback). To defend themselves from attack, kings and nobles often lived in strong castles, with thick stone walls. Some castles were so strong they have lasted until today.

'Gothic' architecture was a great invention of the Middle Ages. This is a 'gargoyle' on Milan Cathedral.

Christianity became the main religion in Europe during the Middle Ages, and churches were built almost everywhere. Some of them are very impressive – especially the great cathedrals, with their tall towers and colourful stained-glass windows.

Monks were involved in farming and helped develop agriculture all over Europe. They also set up schools and wrote books. Their monasteries often had libraries where important books from ancient times were preserved.

In southern Spain, where Islam was the main religion, the rulers built beautiful mosques and minarets. The most famous ones left today are the mosque in Cordoba and the Giralda minaret in Seville.

View of the huge medieval mosque in Cordoba (Spain).

The Renaissance
roughly 1300 to 1600 AD

During the Middle Ages, most people could not read or write and they knew only what they learnt in church. Only monasteries and universities had copies of the books the ancient Greeks and Romans had written. But in the 1300s and 1400s, students began rediscovering the ancient books. They were amazed at the great ideas and knowledge they found there and the news began to spread.

Wealthy and educated people, for example in Florence (Italy), became very interested. They could afford to buy books – especially once printing was invented in Europe (1445) – and they fell in love with ancient Greece and Rome. They had their homes modelled on Roman palaces, and they paid talented artists and sculptors to decorate them with scenes from Greek and Roman stories, and with statues of gods, heroes and emperors.

One of the world's most famous statues: David by Michelangelo.

Leonardo da Vinci designed this 'helicopter' 500 years ago!

One of the great Renaissance paintings: Venus by Botticelli.

It was as if a lost world of beauty and wisdom had been reborn. That is why we call this period the 'Renaissance' (meaning 'rebirth').

It gave the world:

> great painters and sculptors such as Michelangelo and Botticelli;
> talented architects like Brunelleschi;
> the amazing inventor and artist Leonardo da Vinci;
> great thinkers such as Thomas More, Erasmus and Montaigne;
> scientists such as Copernicus and Galileo (who discovered that the Earth and other planets move around the sun);
> beautiful buildings such as the castles in the Loire valley;
> a new interest in what human beings can achieve.

The Industrial Revolution
roughly 1750 to 1880 AD

A new revolution started in Europe about 250 years ago – in the world of 'industry'. It all began with an energy crisis. For thousands of years, people had been burning wood and charcoal. But now, parts of Europe were running out of forests! What else could we use as fuel?

The answer was coal. There was plenty of it in Europe, and miners began digging for it. Coal powered the newly invented steam engines. It could also be roasted and turned into 'coke', which is a much cleaner fuel – ideal for making iron and steel.

About 150 years ago, an Englishman called Henry Bessemer invented a 'blast furnace' that could produce large amounts of steel quite cheaply. Soon Europe was producing huge quantities of it, and it changed the world! Cheap steel made it possible to build skyscrapers, huge bridges, ocean liners, cars, fridges… Powerful guns and bombs too.

Wikimedia

Henry Bessemer – the inventor of modern steelmaking.

Great discoveries and new ideas
roughly 1500 to 1900 AD

Replicas of Christopher Columbus's ships.

Vasco da Gama – the first man to sail from Europe to India.

The dodo, a flightless bird, once lived on an island in the Indian Ocean. It was driven to extinction by European colonists.

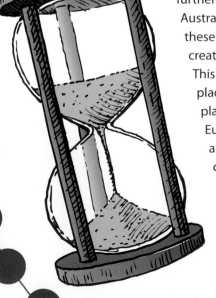
Voltaire, one of the great writers of the Enlightenment age.

At the time of the Renaissance, trade with distant lands was becoming very important for European merchants. For example, they were selling goods in India and bringing back valuable spices and precious stones. But travelling overland was difficult and took a long time, so the merchants wanted to reach India by sea. The problem was, Africa was in the way – and it is very big!

However, if the world really was round (as people were beginning to believe), European ships ought to be able to reach India by sailing west. So, in 1492, Christopher Columbus and his sailors set out from Spain and crossed the Atlantic. But instead of reaching India they discovered the Bahamas (islands in the Caribbean Sea, near the coast of America).

Other explorers soon followed. In 1497–98, Vasco da Gama – a Portuguese naval officer – was the first European to reach India by sailing around Africa. In 1519, another Portuguese explorer – Ferdinand Magellan, working for the King of Spain – led the first European expedition to sail right round the world!

Before long, Europeans were exploring the Caribbean islands and America (which they called the 'New World') and founding colonies there. In other words, they took over the land, claiming it now belonged to their home country in Europe. They took their beliefs, customs and languages with them – and that is how English and French came to be the main languages spoken in North America, and Spanish and Portuguese in Central and South America.

As time passed, Europeans sailed further and further – to China, Japan, South-East Asia, Australia and Oceania. Sailors returning from these distant lands reported seeing strange creatures very different from those in Europe. This made scientists keen to explore these places and to bring back animals and plants for Europe's museums. In the 1800s, European explorers went deep into Africa and by 1910 European nations had colonised most of the African continent.

Meanwhile, back in Europe, scientists were finding out more and more about about how the universe works. Geologists, studying rocks and fossils, began wondering how the Earth had been formed and how old it really was. Two great scientists, Jean-Baptiste Lamarck (in France) and Charles Darwin (in England), eventually concluded that animals and plants had 'evolved' – changing from one species into another over millions and millions of years.

In the 1700s, people were asking other important questions too – such as how countries should be governed, and what rights and freedoms people should have. The writer Jean-Jacques Rousseau said that everyone should be equal. Another writer, Voltaire, said the world would be better if reason and knowledge replaced ignorance and superstition.

This age of new ideas, called the 'Enlightenment', led to great changes in some countries – for example the French revolution of 1789, when the people decided they would no longer be ruled by kings and queens. One of their revolutionary slogans was 'freedom, equality and brotherhood' – which eventually became the French national motto.

©Julia Margaret Cameron

Charles Darwin published his theory of evolution in 1859.

©Zubro Wikimedia

The first telephone – invented by Scottish-born Alexander Graham Bell. Today, Europe makes the latest mobile phones.

The modern world
roughly 1880 until today

Other European inventions from the 19th and 20th centuries helped create the world we know today. For example:

1886	*The petrol engine*	1912	*Neon lighting*	1937	*Instant coffee*
1901	*First radio messages*	1920s	*Television and motorways*	1939	*First jet aircraft*
1909	*Bakelite, the first plastic*	1935	*Radar and the biro pen*	1940s	*First computer*

Today, roughly a quarter of the people working in Europe are producing things needed for the modern world: food and drinks; mobile phones and computers; clothes and furniture; washing machines and televisions; cars, buses and lorries and lots more besides.

About 7 out of every 10 European workers have 'service' jobs. In other words, they work in shops and post offices, banks and insurance companies, hotels and restaurants, hospitals and schools, etc. – either selling things or providing services that people need.

27

Learning the lessons of history

Sadly, the story of Europe is not all about great achievements we can be proud of. There are also many things to be ashamed of. Down the centuries, European nations fought terrible wars against each other. These wars were usually about power and property, or religion.

European colonists killed millions of native people on other continents – by fighting or mistreating them, or by accidentally spreading European diseases among them. Europeans also took millions of Africans to work as slaves.

Lessons had to be learnt from these dreadful wrongdoings. The European slave trade was abolished in the 1800s. Colonies gained their freedom in the 1900s. And peace did come to Europe at last.

To find out how, read the chapter called 'Bringing the family together: the story of the European Union'.

War

Regrettably, there have been many quarrels in the European family. Often they were about who should rule a country, or which country owned which piece of land. Sometimes a ruler wanted to gain more power by conquering his neighbours, or to prove that his people were stronger and better than other peoples.

One way or another, for hundreds of years, there were terrible wars in Europe. In the 20th century, two big wars started on this continent but spread and involved countries all around the world. That is why they are called world wars. They killed millions of people and left Europe poor and in ruins.

Could anything be done to stop these things happening again? Would Europeans ever learn to sit down together and discuss things instead of fighting?

The answer is 'yes'.

That's the story of our next chapter: the story of the European Union.

and peace

We Europeans belong to many different countries, with different languages, traditions, customs and beliefs. Yet we belong together, like a big family, for all sorts of reasons.

Here are some of them.

> We have shared this continent for thousands of years.

> Our languages are often related to one another.

> Many people in every country are descended from people from other countries.

> Our traditions, customs and festivals often have the same origins.

> We share and enjoy the beautiful music and art, and the many plays and stories, that people from all over Europe have given us, down the centuries.

> Almost everyone in Europe believes in things like fair play, neighbourliness, freedom to have your own opinions, respect for each other and caring for people in need.

> So we enjoy what's different and special about our own country and region, but we also enjoy what we have in common as Europeans.

29

The story of the European Union

The Second World War ended in 1945. It had been a time of terrible destruction and killing, and it had started in Europe. How could the leaders of European countries stop such dreadful things from ever happening again? They needed a really good plan that had never been tried before.

Robert Schuman.

Jean Monnet.

A brand new idea

A Frenchman called Jean Monnet thought hard about this. He realised that there were two things a country needed before it could make war: iron for producing steel (to make tanks, guns, bombs and so on) and coal to provide the energy for factories and railways. Europe had plenty of coal and steel: that's why European countries had easily been able to make weapons and go to war.

So Jean Monnet came up with a very daring new idea. His idea was that the governments of France and Germany – and perhaps of other European countries too – should no longer run their own coal and steel industries. Instead, these industries should be organised by people from all the countries involved, and they would sit around a table and discuss and decide things together. That way, war between them would be impossible!

Jean Monnet felt that his plan really would work if only European leaders were willing to try it. He spoke about it to his friend Robert Schuman, who was a minister in the French government. Robert Schuman thought it was a brilliant idea and he announced it in an important speech on 9 May 1950.

The speech convinced not only the French and German leaders but also the leaders of Belgium, Italy, Luxembourg and the Netherlands. They all decided to put their coal and steel industries together and to form a club they called the European Coal and Steel Community (ECSC). It would work for peaceful purposes and help rebuild Europe from the ruins of war. The ECSC was set up in 1951.

Bored at the border…
Queues like this used to
be part of normal life in
Europe.

The common market

The six countries got on so well working together that they soon decided to start another club, called the European Economic Community (EEC). It was set up in 1957.

'Economic' means 'to do with the economy' – in other words, to do with money, business, jobs and trade.

One of the main ideas was that the EEC countries would share a 'common market', to make it easier to trade together. Until then, lorries and trains and barges carrying goods from one country to another always had to stop at the border, and papers had to be checked and money called 'customs duties' had to be paid. This held things up and made goods from abroad more expensive.

The point of having a common market was to get rid of all those border checks and delays and customs duties, and to allow countries to trade with one another just as if they were all one single country.

Food and farming

Machines like this are
used to harvest wheat
and other crops.

The Second World War had made it very difficult for Europe to produce food or to import it from other continents. Europe was short of food even in the early 1950s. So the EEC decided on an arrangement for paying its farmers to produce more food, and to make sure that they could earn a decent living from the land.

This arrangement was called the 'common agricultural policy' (or CAP). It worked well. So well, in fact, that farmers ended up producing too much food and the arrangement had to be changed! Nowadays, the CAP also pays farmers to look after the countryside.

From EEC to European Union

The common market was soon making life easier for people in the EEC.

They had more money to spend, more food to eat and more varied things in their shops. Other neighbouring countries saw this and, in the 1960s, some of them began asking whether they too could join the club.

After years of discussions, the United Kingdom, Denmark and Ireland joined in 1973. It was the turn of Greece in 1981, followed by Portugal and Spain in 1986, and Austria, Finland and Sweden in 1995.

Joining the club. In this picture, Greece signs up for membership.

So now the club had 15 members.

Over these years, the club was changing. By the end of 1992 it had finished building the 'single market' (as it became known), and it was doing a lot more besides. For example, EEC countries were working together to protect the environment and to build better roads and railways right across Europe. Richer countries helped poorer ones with their road building and other important projects.

To make life easier for travellers, most EEC countries had got rid of passport checks at the borders between them. A person living in one member country was free to go and live and find work in any other member country. The governments were discussing other new ideas too – for example, how policemen from different countries could help one another catch criminals, drug smugglers and terrorists.

In short, the club was so different and so much more united that, in 1992, it decided to change its name to the 'European Union' (EU).

Protecting the environment includes reducing air pollution – for example, using wind energy to make electricity.

A policeman and his dog check luggage for drugs.

Bringing the family together

Meanwhile, exciting things were happening beyond the EU's borders. For many years, the eastern and western parts of Europe had been kept apart. The rulers in the eastern part believed in a system of government called 'Communism', which resulted in a hard life for the population there. People were oppressed, and many of those who spoke up against the regime were sent to prison.

When more and more people fled from the east to the west, rulers in the east became afraid. They erected tall fences and high walls, like the one in Berlin, to prevent people from leaving their countries. Many who tried to cross the border without permission were shot. The separation was so powerful that it was often described as an 'Iron Curtain'.

Finally, in 1989, the separation ended. The Berlin Wall was knocked down and the 'Iron Curtain' ceased to exist. Soon, Germany was reunited. The peoples of the central and eastern parts of Europe chose for themselves new governments that got rid of the old, strict Communist system.

They were free at last! It was a wonderful time of celebration.

1989: demolishing the Berlin Wall.

The countries that had gained freedom began asking whether they could join the European Union, and soon there was quite a queue of 'candidate' countries waiting to become EU members.

Before a country can join the European Union, its economy has to be working well. It also has to be democratic – in other words, its people must be free to choose who they want to govern them. And it must respect human rights. Human rights include the right to say what you think, the right not to be put in prison without a fair trial, the right not to be tortured, and many other important rights as well.

The former Communist countries worked hard at all these things and, after a few years, eight of them were ready: the Czech Republic, Estonia, Hungary, Latvia, Lithuania, Poland, Slovakia and Slovenia.

They joined the EU on 1 May 2004, along with two Mediterranean islands – Cyprus and Malta. On 1 January 2007, two more former Communist countries, Bulgaria and Romania, joined the group. Croatia joined the EU on 1 July 2013, bringing the total to 28 countries.

Never before have so many countries joined the EU in such a short time. This is a real 'family reunion', bringing together the eastern, central and western parts of Europe.

The flags of the 28 members of the EU.

What the EU does

The EU tries to make life better in all sorts of ways. Here are some of them.

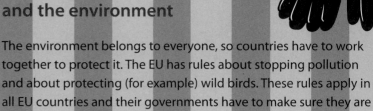

Climate change and the environment

The environment belongs to everyone, so countries have to work together to protect it. The EU has rules about stopping pollution and about protecting (for example) wild birds. These rules apply in all EU countries and their governments have to make sure they are obeyed.

Climate change – also known as global warming – is another problem that countries cannot tackle alone. EU countries have therefore agreed to work together to lower the amount of emissions they produce that harm the atmosphere and cause global warming. The EU is also trying to influence other countries to do the same.

Pollution crosses borders, so European countries work together to protect the environment.

The euro

The euro is used in many EU countries.

In years gone by, each country in Europe had its own kind of money, or 'currency'. Now there is one single currency, the euro, which all EU countries can introduce if they are ready for it. Having one currency makes it easier to do business and to travel and shop all over the EU without having to change from one currency to another. Today, more than two thirds of the EU's citizens are using the euro instead of the old currencies.

If you compare euro coins you will see that on one side there is a design representing the country it was made in. The other side is the same for all the countries.

Freedom!

Students from different countries study together, with help from the EU.

People in the EU are free to live, work or study in whichever EU country they choose, and the EU is doing all it can to make it simple to move home from one country to another. When you cross the borders between most EU countries, you no longer need a passport. The EU encourages students and young people to spend some time studying or training in another European country.

Jobs

It's important for people to have jobs that they enjoy and are good at. Some of the money they earn goes to pay for hospitals and schools, and to look after old people. That's why the EU is doing all it can to create new and better jobs for everyone who can work. It helps people to set up new businesses, and provides money to train people to do new kinds of work.

Training people to do new jobs is very important.

Helping regions in difficulty

Life is not easy for everyone everywhere in Europe. In some places there are not enough jobs for people, because mines or factories have closed down. In some areas, farming is hard because of the climate, or trade is difficult because there are not enough roads and railways.

The EU tackles these problems by collecting money from all its member countries and using it to help regions that are in difficulty. For example, it helps pay for new roads and rail links, and it helps businesses to provide new jobs for people.

The EU helps pay for new roads.

Helping poor countries

In many countries around the world, people are dying or living difficult lives because of war, disease and natural disasters such as droughts or floods. Often these countries do not have enough money to build the schools and hospitals, roads and houses that their people need.

The EU gives money to these countries, and sends teachers, doctors, engineers and other experts to work there. It also buys many things that those countries produce without charging customs duties. That way, the poor countries can earn more money.

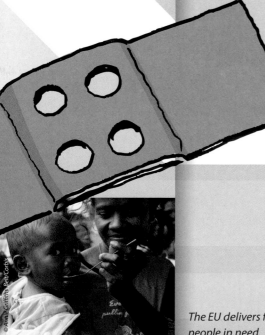

The EU delivers food to people in need.

The European flag.

Peace

The European Union has brought many European countries together in friendship. Of course, they don't always agree on everything but, instead of fighting, their leaders sit round a table to sort out their disagreements.

So the dream of Jean Monnet and Robert Schuman has come true.

The EU has brought peace among its members. It is also working for lasting peace among its neighbours and in the wider world. For example, EU soldiers and police officers are helping keep the peace in the former Yugoslavia, where there was bitter fighting not many years ago.

These are just some of the things the EU does: there are many more. In fact, being in the European Union makes a difference to just about every aspect of our lives. What things should the EU be doing, or not doing? That's for the people in the EU to decide. How can we have our say? Find out in the next chapter.

Europe has its own flag and its own anthem – *Ode to Joy* from Beethoven's ninth symphony. The original words are in German, but when used as the European anthem it has no words – only the tune. You can hear it on the Internet:

europa.eu/about-eu/basic-information/symbols/anthem/index_en.htm

Here is a list of some famous European landmarks:

1. Atomium, Brussels, Belgium
2. Stonehenge, Wiltshire, United Kingdom
3. Royal Monastery of San Lorenzo de El Escorial, Madrid, Spain
4. The Parthenon, Athens, Greece
5. Parliament Building, Budapest, Hungary
6. Eiffel Tower, Paris, France
7. Windmills, the Netherlands
8. Charles Bridge, Prague, Czech Republic
9. The Little Mermaid statue, Copenhagen, Denmark
10. Church of St Nicholas, Sofia, Bulgaria
11. Sagrada Familia Cathedral, Barcelona, Spain
12. The Colosseum, Rome, Italy
13. Brandenburg Gate, Berlin, Germany

Can you find each of them on the map below?
The previous page might help you!

The European Union countries

The countries are in alphabetical order according to what each country is called in its own language or languages (as shown in brackets).

Flag	Country	Capital city	Population
	Belgium (Belgique/België)	Brussels (Brussel/Bruxelles)	11.2 million
	Bulgaria (България/Bulgaria)	Sofia (София/Sofija)	7.3 million
	Czech Republic (Česká republika)	Prague (Praha)	10.5 million
	Denmark (Danmark)	Copenhagen (København)	5.6 million
	Germany (Deutschland)	Berlin (Berlin)	80.5 million
	Estonia (Eesti)	Tallinn (Tallinn)	1.3 million
	Ireland (Éire/Ireland)	Dublin (Baile Atha Cliath/Dublin)	4.6 million
	Greece (Ελλάδα/Elláda)	Athens (Αθήνα/Athinai)	11.1 million
	Spain (España)	Madrid (Madrid)	46.7 million
	France (France)	Paris (Paris)	65.6 million
	Croatia (Hrvatska)	Zagreb (Zagreb)	4.3 million
	Italy (Italia)	Rome (Roma)	59.7 million
	Cyprus (Κύπρος/Kypros) (Kibris)	Nicosia (Λευκωσία/Lefkosia) (Lefkosa)	0.9 million
	Latvia (Latvija)	Riga (Riga)	2.0 million
	Lithuania (Lietuva)	Vilnius (Vilnius)	3.0 million
	Luxembourg (Luxemburg)	Luxembourg (Luxemburg)	0.5 million
	Hungary (Magyarország)	Budapest (Budapest)	9.9 million
	Malta (Malta)	Valletta (Valletta)	0.4 million
	Netherlands (Nederland)	Amsterdam (Amsterdam)	16.8 million
	Austria (Österreich)	Vienna (Wien)	8.5 million
	Poland (Polska)	Warsaw (Warszawa)	38.5 million
	Portugal (Portugal)	Lisbon (Lisboa)	10.5 million
	Romania (România)	Bucharest (Bucureşti)	20.1 million
	Slovenia (Slovenija)	Ljubljana (Ljubljana)	2.1 million
	Slovakia (Slovensko)	Bratislava (Bratislava)	5.4 million
	Finland (Suomi/Finland)	Helsinki (Helsinki/Helsingfors)	5.4 million
	Sweden (Sverige)	Stockholm (Stockholm)	9.6 million
	United Kingdom (*) (United Kingdom)	London (London)	63.9 million

(*) The full name of this country is 'the United Kingdom of Great Britain and Northern Ireland', but for short most people just call it Britain, the United Kingdom or the UK.

Population figures are for 2013.
Source: Eurostat

Let's explore Europe! Quiz

(Hint: you can find the answers to all these questions in this booklet)

1. How many continents are there in the world?

2. Which two cities does the Channel Tunnel connect?

3. What do you call it when birds fly south in autumn and spend the winter in warmer regions?

4. What do you call it when farmers water their fields with water from the ground or rivers?

5. Name a type of marine animal that can be farmed.

6. What does 'democracy' mean?

7. Which material, used to power steam engines, made the Industrial Revolution possible?

8. Which historic event took place in 1789?

9. In which decade was the computer invented?

10. How many countries are part of the European Union?

11. Where is the EU Court of Justice based?

12. How often do European elections take place?

Want to play games, test your knowledge and explore Europe further?
Go to: europa.eu/europago/explore

Answers: 1. Seven (Europe, Africa, North and South America, Antarctica, Asia and Australia/Oceania) (p. 3) / 2. Calais in France and Folkestone in England (p. 6) / 3. Migration (p. 11) / 4. Irrigation (p. 13) / 5. Salmon, mussels, oysters, clams (p. 17) / 6. Government by the people (p. 20) / 7. Coal (p. 25) / 8. The French Revolution (p. 27) / 9. 1940s (p. 27) / 10. 28 / 11. Luxembourg (p. 41) / 12. Every five years (p. 40)

Ministers from all EU governments meet to pass EU laws.

How the EU takes decisions

As you can imagine, it takes a lot of effort by a lot of people to organise the EU and make everything work. Who does what?

The European Commission

In Brussels, a group of women and men (one from each EU country) meet every Wednesday to discuss what needs to be done next. These people are put forward by the government of their country but approved by the European Parliament.

They are called 'commissioners', and together they make up the European Commission. Their job is to think about what would be best for the EU as a whole, and to propose new laws for the EU as a whole. In their work they are helped by experts, lawyers, secretaries, translators and so on.

Once they have agreed what law to propose, they send their proposal to the European Parliament and the Council of the European Union.

The European Parliament

The European Parliament represents all the people in the EU. It holds a big meeting every month, in Strasbourg (France), to discuss and decide the new laws being proposed by the European Commission.

There are 751 members of the European Parliament (MEPs). They are chosen, every five years, in an election when all the adult citizens of the EU get the chance to vote. By choosing our MEP, and by talking to him or her, we can have a say in what the EU decides to do.

The European Council

This is where all the leaders of the EU countries get together regularly at 'summit meetings', to talk about how things are going in Europe and to set the strategy for Europe. They don't discuss things in great detail, such as how to word new laws.

The Council

New laws for Europe have to be discussed by government ministers from all the EU countries, not only by the members of the European Parliament. When the ministers meet together they are called 'the Council'.

After discussing a proposal, the Council votes on it. There are rules about how many votes each country has, and how many are needed to pass a law. In some cases, the rule says the Council has to be in complete agreement.

Once the Council and the Parliament have passed a new law, EU countries have to respect it.

The Court of Justice

If a country doesn't apply the law properly, the European Commission will warn it and may complain about it to the Court of Justice, in Luxembourg. The Court's job is to make sure that EU laws are respected, and are applied in the same way everywhere. It has one judge from each EU country.

There are other groups of people (committees of experts and so on) involved in taking decisions in the EU, because it's important to get them right.

Tomorrow...

One of the challenges facing Europe today is how to make sure that young people can have jobs and a good future. It's not easy, because European firms have to compete for business with companies in other parts of the world that may be able to do the same job more cheaply.

There are other big problems today which can only be tackled by countries around the world working together, for example:

> pollution and climate change;
> hunger and poverty;
> international crime and terrorism.

The European Union is working on these problems, but it's not always easy for so many different governments and the European Parliament to agree on what to do. It doesn't help that the EU's decision-making rules are rather complicated.

What's more, many people feel that just voting for their MEP once every five years doesn't give them much of a say in what gets decided in Brussels or Strasbourg.

... and beyond

So we need to make sure that everyone can have their say in what the European Union decides.

How can we do that? Do you have any good ideas? What are the most important problems you think the EU should be dealing with, and what would you like it to do about them?

Why not discuss and jot down your ideas with your teacher and your classmates and send them to your MEP? You can find out who he or she is and where to write to them on the following website: europarl.europa.eu/

You can also contact the European Commission or Parliament at one of the addresses at the end of this book and perhaps even arrange for your class to visit the two institutions.

We are today's European children: before long we'll be Europe's adults.

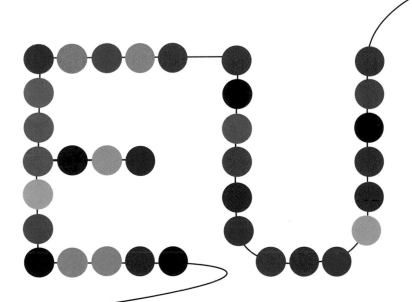

The future is for us to decide – together!

Useful links

For you & For your teacher

Why not test what you have learned in this book and play the Let's explore Europe game online?

Go to:
europa.eu/europago/explore

Kid's Corner

You can find out fun facts about each of the EU countries and learn more about the EU on Kids' Corner. It's packed with games and quizzes too!

europa.eu/kids-corner

Teachers' Corner

The European Union's online Teachers' Corner is a one-stop resource centre for a wide range of teaching material about the European Union and its policies.
The material has been produced by various EU institutions and other government and non-government bodies. Whether you're looking for inspiration for your lessons or for existing educational material about European history and culture, or even specific topics such as climate change and reducing energy consumption, you should find something useful tailored to the age group of your pupils at the following address:

europa.eu/teachers-corner